BIRDS
COLORING BOOK
FOR ADULTS

AN ADULT COLORING BOOK OF 40 BIRDS IN A RANGE OF STYLES AND ORNATE PATTERNS

ADULT COLORING WORLD

ISBN-13: 978-1522721192

ISBN-10: 1522721193

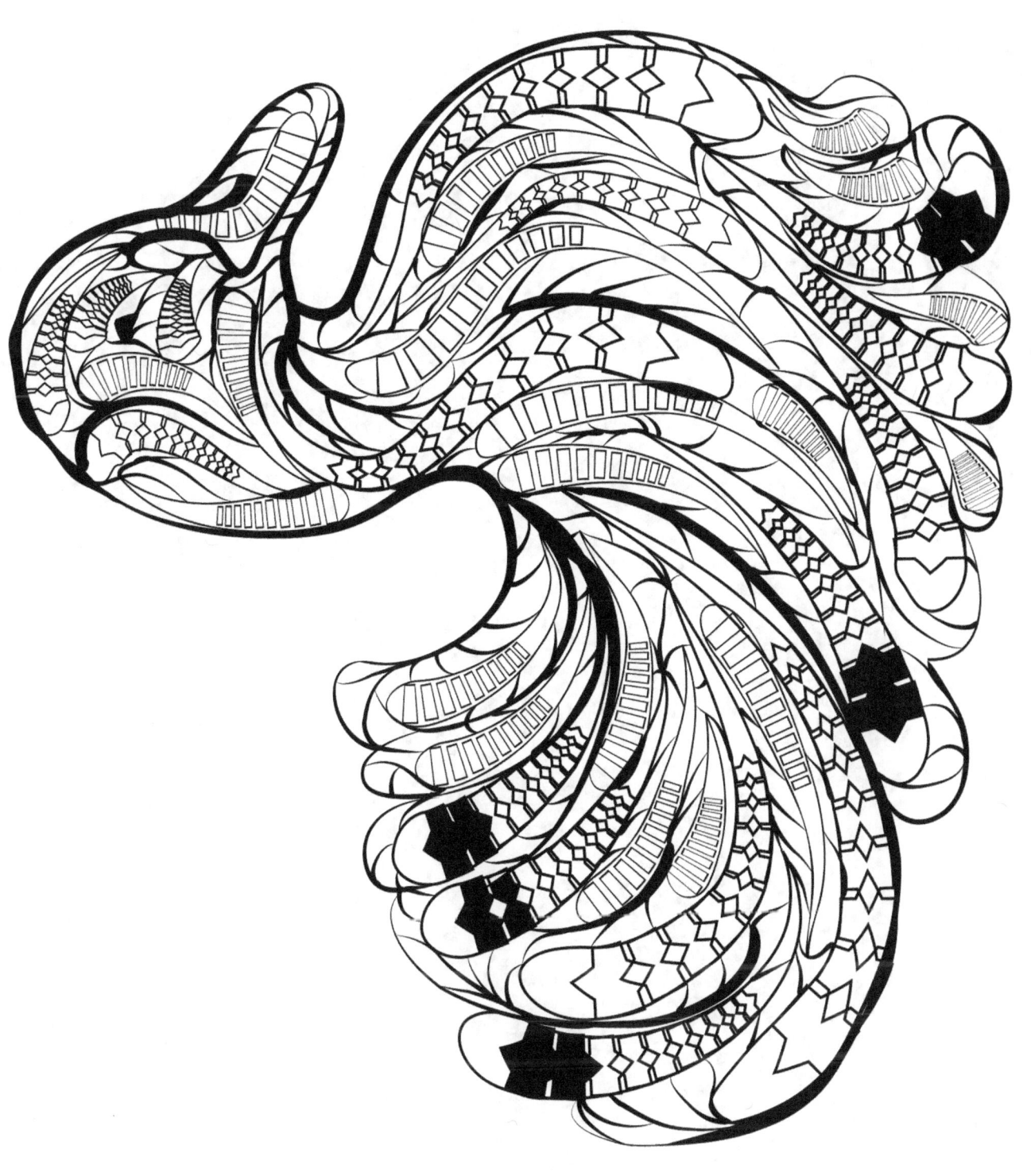

www.ingramcontent.com/pod-product-compliance
Lightning Source LLC
Chambersburg PA
CBHW081235280526
45787CB00006B/2669